CW01594078

LET'S INVESTIGATE

LEARNING TO RIDE

Published in this edition by Peter Haddock Ltd,
Pinfold Lane, Bridlington, East Yorkshire, YO16 5BT

© 1997 Peter Haddock Ltd/Geddes & Grosset Ltd

All rights reserved. No part of this publication may be reproduced, stored in a retrieval system, or transmitted, in any form or by any means, electronic, mechanical, photocopying, recording or otherwise without the prior permission of the copyright holder.

ISBN 0 7105 0982 0

Printed and bound in India

PART ONE

FINDING WHERE TO RIDE

You are thinking of learning to ride. What is the best age to start? Since you are old enough to read this you are already old enough to ride. Some parents put their children on a pony almost before they can walk, but this is not learning to ride. If you try to match your strength against a horse, or even the smallest pony, you will surely lose. Few children have the strength to start learning to ride until they are about six or seven.

Where do you go to learn? For a long time there was no control over riding schools. Anyone with a horse or pony, which might be quite unsuitable, could open a 'riding school'. There is now some control by local authorities over riding schools, but this is mainly to ensure that the ponies and horses are not ill-treated. It does not cover the ability of the instructors to teach riding; and bad habits, once learned, are hard to forget, as well as possibly being dangerous.

Project

Get a list

The first thing to do is to write to the British Horse Society, at the British Equestrian Centre, Stoneleigh

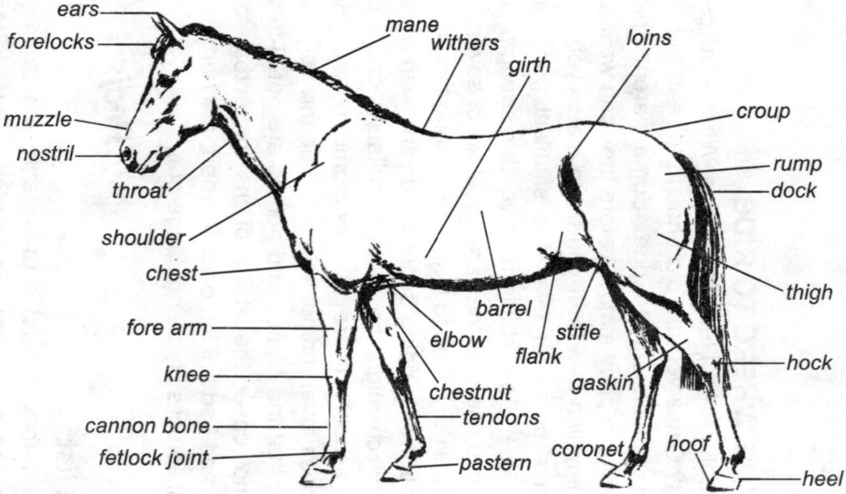

Figure 1: the points of a horse

Park, Kenilworth, Warwickshire CV8 2LR (telephone 01203 696 697), for a list of approved schools.

If there is an approved riding school that is within reasonable distance of your home, then many of your problems about starting are easily solved. The BHS list shows also what facilities the schools have, and in which branches of horsemanship, such as show jumping, preparation for hunting, and so on, they may specialise.

Having decided on a few possible schools, go to see them. Although they may all be good, it is likely that one will be more suitable for you than others.

Project

How did it look?

The school may look something like figures 2a and 2b. After visiting each one, write down your main thoughts. Was the stable yard tidy, without odd buckets, pitchforks and wisps of straw all over it? Did the ponies seem quiet and contented? Was there a general air of chaos or of organisation? Did the people who worked there appear to be the sort of people you would get along with and have confidence in?

Have a look around outside the stables to see what land, if any, the school has. The best place to start learning to ride, as well as to start training a young horse or pony, is in a small paddock. Quite often, especially in cities, riding schools may have no land, which means

Figure 2a: Plan of a riding school

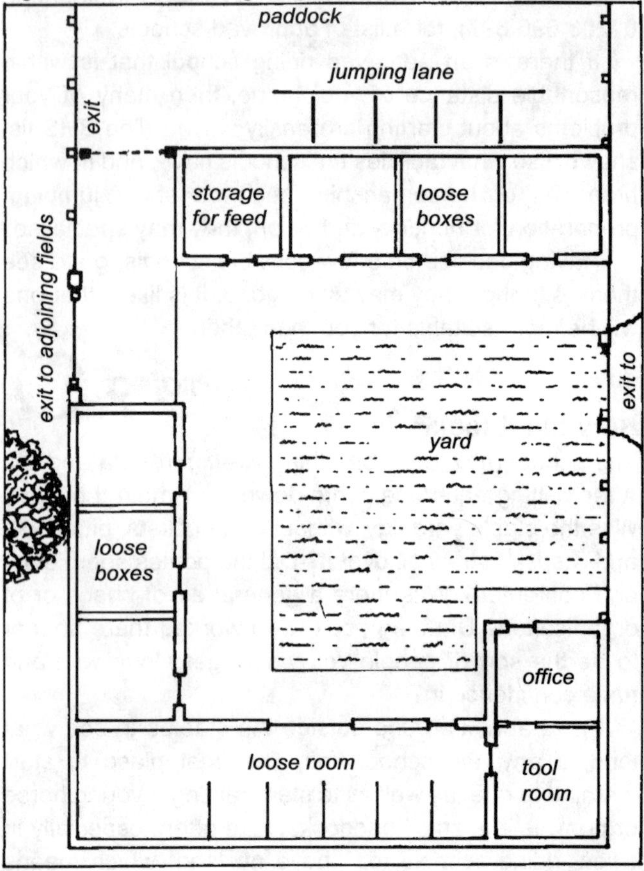

Figure 2b: A riding school

that the first time you go out on a pony you will be on a road. This should not automatically stop you going to that school if everything else is satisfactory, but it is a disadvantage to be considered.

If you are lucky enough to have a choice of two or three schools that you think look suitable, work out how you are going to get to each of them, and how long it is going to take. This may not matter much during summer holidays, when you will have long days to spare, but it can be important in the autumn and winter, when you want to ride after school.

Another important organisation for teaching young people not only to ride but all about ponies, and how to look after them, is the Pony Club, a subsidiary of the British Horse Society, whose address and phone number are the same.

The Pony Club was formed to encourage youngsters to ride and to learn about ponies. Much of the enjoyment of riding is the stable work that goes with it. You should learn about the tack, that is the name given to the equipment used on a horse. It is important to know about stable routine—even mucking out, which is cleaning out a pony's stall or box. Find out the difference between a stall and a box.

The important and interesting aim of the Pony Club is to help girls and boys to learn about the many different types of pony and horse, what they can and cannot do, and why.

The Club is open to boys and girls under twenty-one. Up to seventeen they are ordinary members, and over that age associate members. There is an annual subscription plus a joining fee, with a new subscription required each October. The Club is split into branches, each covering an area of country, and quite often associated with the hunt there. The branches are very much self-supporting and self-governing, headed by a district commissioner and a committee.

Project

Find out what goes on

Find out the address of your Pony Club branch, then ask the secretary what they do. The Pony Club Rally is usually its most important event. At the ally young Pony Club members have mounted games and are taught riding, care of the horses and about the tack. At the Horse of the Year Show there are finals of these mounted games among teams that have won their way through preliminary rounds.

The Pony Club awards certificates to those who have reached a certain standard in riding, horse-mastership (that is looking after horses), hunting or country lore. Exploring and finding out about the countryside is one of the Pony Club's aims, and it has introduced cross-country treks, non-riding rallies to learn about stable management and care of horses, and the summer camp, which covers a wide field of horse activity.

The Pony Club also publishes a large number of books and pamphlets which you can get by writing to the Secretary of the Pony Club at the British Horse Society address already given on page seven.

Project

Buying the right clothes

You must now consider what to wear. There are one or

two essentials. The first is a hard hat. Some stables have a collection of hard hats for riders to borrow, but it is worthwhile buying a good quality hat of your own that fits well. It is no good having one which looks smart, then falls off when you do.

Some beginners may think that there is something cissy about wearing a hard hat or that it is an admission that they are so insecure that they feel likely to fall off. But a hat is an essential piece of equipment because, no matter how proficient, there has never been a rider who has not fallen off at some time or another. The hat will also protect you from unexpected low branches.

Jodhpurs and boots are best to start with, but, at a pinch, jeans and a pair of stout shoes will do. Thin slacks and high-heeled shoes are completely inappropriate. A riding mackintosh is also part of the rider's essential equipment.

Project

Watch the experts

Other items that go to make an elegant rider can be added as you learn. Watch experienced riders, and make a list of their clothes.

PART TWO

INTO THE SADDLE

Now you are about ready to begin riding. Reading is no substitute for experience in the saddle, but it can help. The first thing to learn when you go to a riding school is patience. Do not rush your pony because this will upset it. At first the pony will be tacked up for you although later you may be allowed to do this for yourself.

Project

First thing to watch

Get to the stable long enough before your first lesson to watch how the saddle and bridle are put on. If the saddle fits correctly, it will be snug but with sufficient clearance of the withers (*see* figure 3) so as not to rub them. The girth should be tight or the saddle may slip, and you with it. Often a horse will blow himself out when the saddle is first put on, so it is important to check that it is tight and to adjust it, if necessary, before mounting. There should be just room for two fingertips under the girth.

Project

The bit to choose

The fitting of the bridle is more involved. There are

Figure 3: The saddle

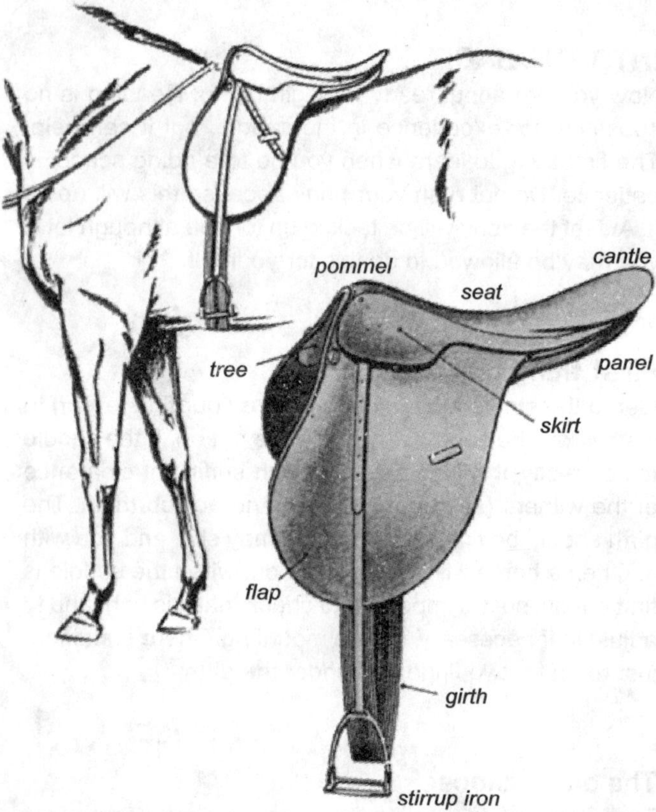

several types of bridle and many different sorts of bit (*see* figure 4). See how many there are in your stable, and find out the reasons why each of them is used. The most common is the snaffle, and probably this is what your first pony will wear. He will have a leading rein. See how this is fitted to give the instructor who is leading you control over your pony's head.

If the instructor is a good one, he or she will not hurry you along at this early stage, so have a good look at your pony, and try to win his confidence. Although he will have done this job many times before, each new rider is a new challenge for him as well as you.

Project

Learning to mount

You must first learn how to mount your pony properly. A noted horseman once said that he could tell how well a person would ride by the way he mounted, and certainly a person who hauls himself or herself up haphazardly and lands with a thump in the saddle is unlikely to have either a good seat or good hands.

When you are experienced, and if you are athletic enough, it may one day be possible for you to vault lightly into the saddle, but for a start the conventional method (*see* figure 5) is to stand on the near side of the pony (the near side is the right side as you face him), and hold the reins in your left, with the off-side rein

Figure 4: Bridles

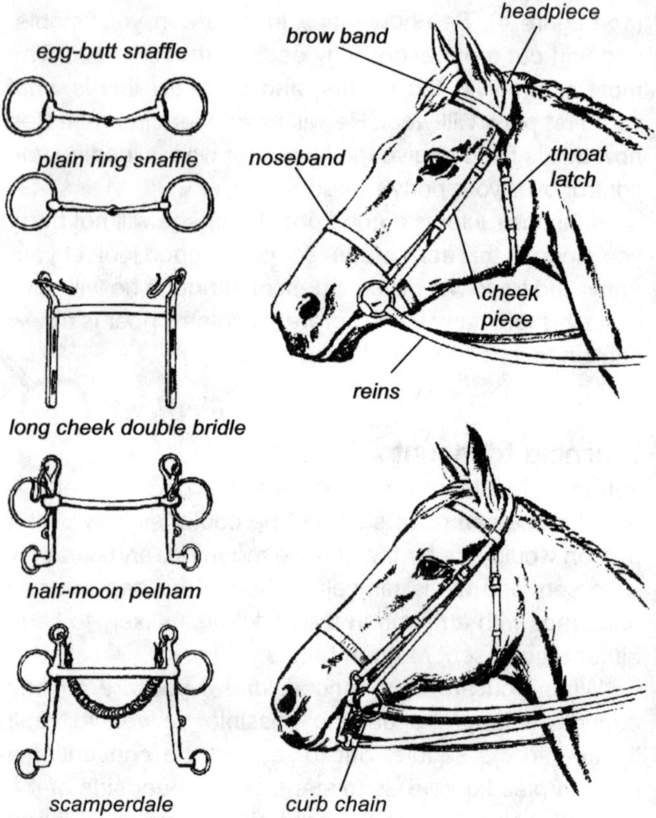

slightly short, to stop the pony taking a crafty nip out of you as you stand facing his tail. With your right hand hold the stirrup iron steady while you put your left foot in it, toe downwards to prevent an unintentional dig in the pony's side. Now hold the pommel (front) of the saddle with your right hand. With a spring off your right foot straighten your left leg so that you are standing in the stirrup, and swing the right leg over the pony's back and into the right stirrup; then lower yourself into the saddle (*see* figure 6).

Dismounting is easier, for you merely take both feet out of the stirrups, swing the right leg over and drop to the ground (*see* figure 7). Some people leave the left foot in the stirrup iron, but if the pony moves off you

Figure 5: How to mount unassisted

back to horse's head with reins in left hand

foot in stirrup

Figure 6

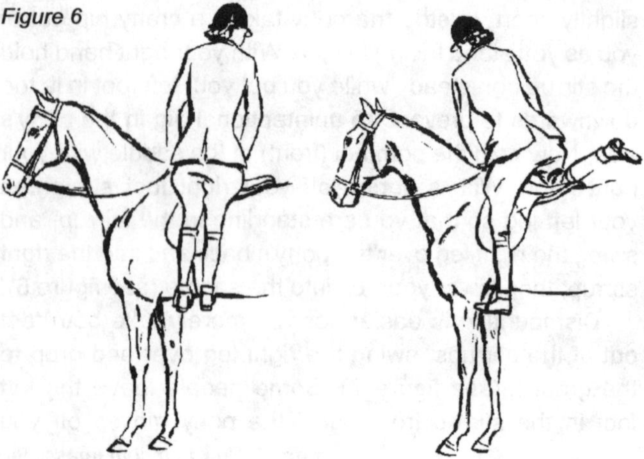

slight pause *and over gently*

could be caught in an awkward or dangerous position. If, because of injury or for some other reason, you must dismount this way, get someone to hold your pony's head for you.

For a start you will probably be led, with the leading rein, but right from the beginning your 'seat' will be formed. The seat is the rider's position in the saddle and determines the rider's own security and much of his or her control over the pony.

Many riders, especially nervous ones, return from their first few rides completely exhausted, with their legs feeling as though they might drop off at any moment.

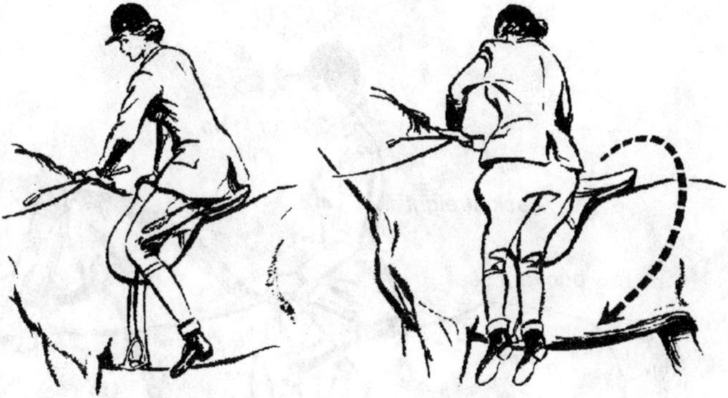

Figure 7: Dismounting

This is because there is a tendency to grip hard the whole time.

A good seat (*see* figure 8) is a mixture of balance, and grip, with balance playing the major part but with an ever-ready awareness to grip when necessary and before the balance has been lost. The reins should not be used as an added means of keeping your balance, and once you are used to the rhythm of the horse, it helps to ride without reins, but still on the leading rein, a lungeing rein or in a free school.

You should be seated well down in the middle of the saddle, with a straight (but never stiff) back and head up,

Figure 8: A good seat

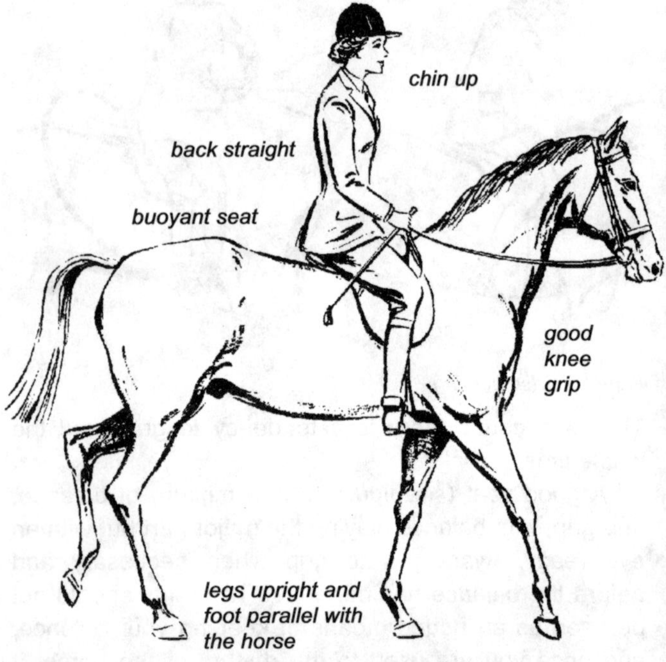

looking straight between your pony's ears. Stiffness in any part of the body should be guarded against, and there are exercises that can be done at home to make the right muscles more supple.

Project

Practise at home

Find a piece of furniture, say the thick arm of a sofa or a small chair, that resembles a saddle. Sit on it and touch each toe with the opposite hand several times in quick succession, bending the body from the waist backwards and then forwards, and in circular movements in each direction; swinging the arms shoulder high diagonally (left in front when right is behind, and vice versa). These exercises are even better sitting on a pony, but make sure it is a quiet one.

Sitting at the trot without stirrups is especially useful at developing a strong, independent seat.

Gripping, when you need to grip, is done with the thigh and the knee, which should at all times be kept close to the saddle, while the lower part of the leg is relaxed (but not flapping in the wind) slightly behind the vertical; the ball of the foot should rest in the stirrup iron, with the heel down and the toes pointing slightly away from the pony's side but not too far.

The strength of a rider's seat depends a great deal upon the length of the stirrup leather. Compare the difference between a flat-race jockey (figure 9) and a dressage rider (figure 10). The stirrup leathers of flat-race jockeys are very short. This means that they have much less grip on the body of the horse.

Figures 9 and 10: Jockey and dressage rider

For the novice and for dressage riders stirrup leather should be long enough to ensure that the rider can use his or her lower leg to give the pony the 'aids' (which we shall come to in Part Three) but not so long as to lose leverage against being pulled forward.

Project

Practise altering the stirrups

At first the stirrups will be adjusted for you, but you are the best guide of what feels right, and so you should practise altering them for yourself, one at a time, and without taking your foot out of the stirrup. A tendency, which is usual, to have the leather too short can be cured by riding without stirrups (cross them over the saddle in front of you) for a while. Automatically, the foot will fall a little lower.

When *walking*, the body should stay in the same position as when at a halt, except for the natural movements caused by the horse.

The *trot* may be ridden either sitting or rising. At a sitting trot the rider retains much more contact with the horse and so is able to maintain more impulsion—which is the suppressed energy of the horse and not be

Figure 11: The trot

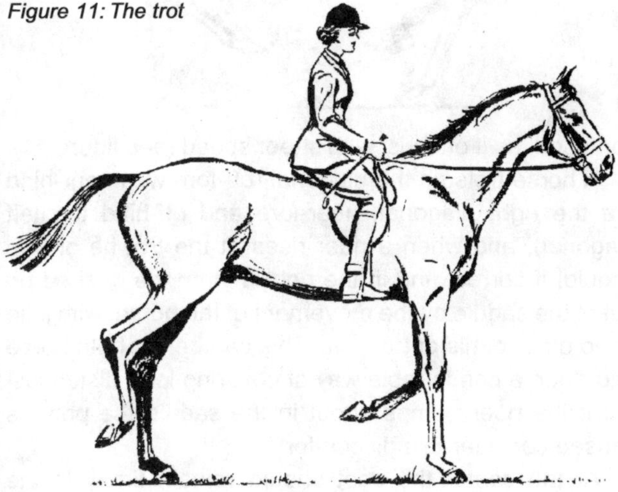

Figure 12: The canter

confused, as it often is, with sheer speed (*see* figure 11).

A horse trots on the diagonal (off-fore with near-hind are the right diagonal; near-fore and off-hind the left diagonal), and when a rider rises at the trot he or she should, if correct and in the right rhythm, be pushed up out of the saddle by the movement of the horse, with little or no effort of his or her own. This can be, for both horse and rider, a comfortable way of covering long distances, but if the rider bumps about in the saddle the pony is caused considerable discomfort.

At the *canter* the seat should remain firmly in the

Figure 13: The gallop

saddle, with the back straight but relaxed in rhythm with the three-beat stride. If the back is stiff the seat is likely to be bumpy, which will be uncomfortable and may well result in damaging the pony's back (*see* figure 12).

The position at the *gallop* will depend very much upon the type of pony or horse one is riding. If he is a reluctant creature, the rider must sit 'into' him and push him along with seat and legs. If, on the other hand, the horse goes along freely, the body is leant forward, with the weight taken on the knees and stirrups. The weight is now over the centre of gravity, and the horse's 'propelling equipment' is left to work untrammelled by his rider (*see* figure 13).

The American jockey Tod Sloan, who lived from 1874-1933 and came to Britain just before the turn of the century, won many races by adopting a crouching style that was dismissed as being 'like a monkey up a stick' until it was realised how effective it was. The Italian Federico Caprilli made the advantages of the 'forward seat' so clear in his training in the Italian cavalry schools and in his writings that it has since been widely adopted both for specialised riding, such as show jumping and steeplechasing, and in everyday riding.

Project

Learn to use your hands

The seat and legs produce the impulsion, which is in turn controlled, as is the direction of the horse, by the hands. These must be so sensitive that it is vital they are completely independent of the seat. A rider who is using his or her reins to 'stay on board' will hardly be able to use them for anything else.

The upper arm should hang loosely by the side, with the forearms and wrist relaxed and supple. Assuming you are using a single rein, it should pass between the little and third finger, and the thumb and forefinger (*see*

Figure 14: Holding the reins

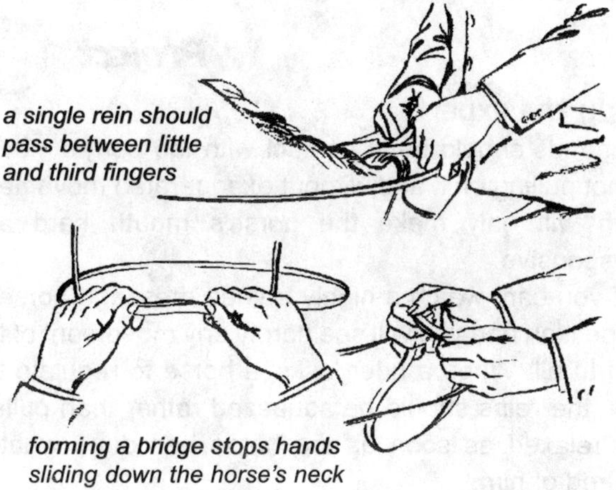

Figure 15: Double bridle

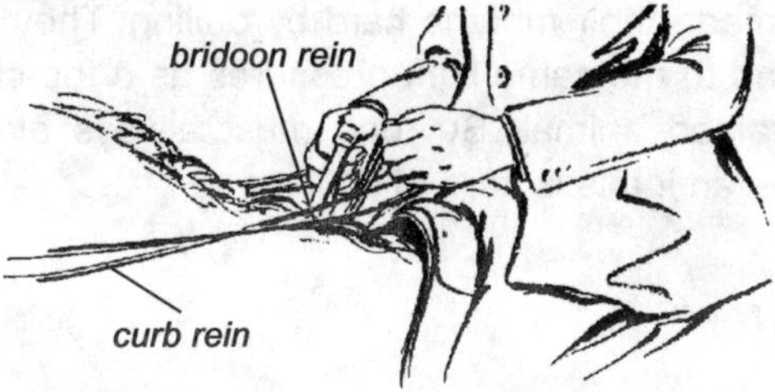

figure 14); with double reins (*see* figure 15), the other rein goes round the little finger.

Project

Study the experts

The hands should be in contact with the pony's mouth, but not pulling on it and without exaggerated movement, which will only make the horse's mouth hard and unresponsive.

If you can, watch a highly trained dressage horse in competition and you will see hardly any movement of the hand at all. When a rider 'asks' a horse to regulate the pace, the reins should be squeezed rather than pulled, then relaxed as soon as the horse has done what is required of him.

This is the ideal, but many riding school horses have for a long time been ridden by inexperienced people who have made their mouths hard by pulling. They may not respond to the same light pressures as a top-class and well-trained animal. But one must always aim at the best, even if this is hard to achieve.

PART THREE

THE AIDS THAT TELL YOUR PONY WHAT TO DO

The 'aids' by which a rider indicates what he wants the pony to do can be divided into the categories of natural and artificial.

The natural aids are the legs, hands, weight of the body, and the voice; the artificial aids are whips, spurs, reins, bits, martingales and so on.

To start a pony walking forward, the reins will be gathered until contact is made with the mouth, and the legs are squeezed until he starts to walk. Again, the mere squeezing may not be enough for a pony possibly used to sterner treatment, in which case you must kick him sharply just behind the girth to produce the required motion.

As well as producing increased pace, the legs are used to direct the hindquarters of a horse, in which case the legs are used independently, according to which way the rider wants the hindquarters to move. The hands control the energy, or impulsion, produced by the legs, the direction of the horse in conjunction with the legs and pace.

The body, in particular the back muscles, will, if

relaxed, help the rider to keep a secure seat and, if straightened, increase the impulsive power of the seat. The weight of the body can be used to help keep a pony balanced on the turn and, if correctly distributed, will if not helping the pony at least not hinder him at the gallop, or while jumping.

Project

Test your voice

Although, obviously, ponies cannot understand the meaning of words, they are sensitive to the tone of the voice, which can be an important factor in soothing a nervous horse, scolding a naughty one, checking an over-bold one, and encouraging a faint-heart. Test the tone of your voice and your pony's reaction.

The use of a whip, or stick, is obvious, although its misuse is too common. Generally, it is a plain or leather-covered cane about 60 centimetres (24 inches) long and carried lightly in the palm, with just a few centimetres extending in front of the hand. It can be used to supplement the leg aids, and a competent rider will be able to use a stick equally well with either hand.

The stick should be applied firmly, and, as with the natural aids, only for as long as needed to produce the required result. It may be used to punish a wilfully disobedient horse—although first be sure the horse knows what is wanted of him—and then it must be done firmly but never in anger. The horse should be hit behind the leg and *never on the head.*

Longer whips are used for schooling and for lungeing (*see* figure 16), while the hunting whip is specially designed not only for dealing with the horse but also with hounds and with other eventualities such as the need to open and close gates.

Figure: 16 Lungeing

Project

Count your spurs

There are many different types of spur, and some, especially types used in older times, were sharply pointed and very cruel. See how many kinds you can find in old pictures.

Spurs should be used as an addition to the leg 'aid' and not as a substitute by riders too lazy or unable to use the leg properly. Indeed, they should not be used until a rider is completely in control of his or her legs. The spurs should have blunt ends and, if curved, the curved ends should point downwards.

Project

Count the bridles

Although there is a considerable variety of bits and bridles, there are five main groups: the snaffle, double bridle, pelham, gag and the bitless bridle (*see* figure 4).

The snaffle is the simplest and most commonly used type, and there are several variations of it. See how many are used in your riding school or Pony Club branch. The double bridle gives the experienced horse rider a greater degree of control over his or her horse, and is therefore popular in the show ring, where a horse needs to be displayed to the best effect.

Figure 17: The martingale

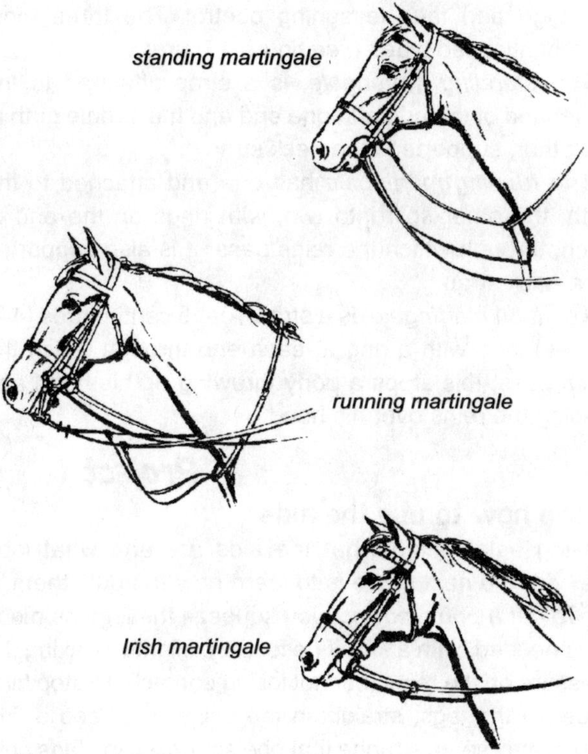

The martingale is a strap that runs from the reins to the girth that prevents the horse from carrying his head too high and thus lessening control. The three most commonly used types (*see* figure 17) are:

1 The *standing martingale*, is a strap attached to the noseband of the bridle at one end and the saddle girth at the other, supported by a neck strap.

2 The *running martingale* has one end attached to the girth, the other split into two, with rings on the end of each, through which the reins pass. It is also supported by a neck strap.

3 The *Irish martingale*, is a strap 10–15 centimetres (4–6 inches) long with a ring at each end through which the reins pass; this stops a pony throwing up his head and tossing the reins over his head.

Project

Learn how to use the aids

Having established what the aids are and what jobs they do, the next move is to learn how to apply them.

To get a pony moving, you squeeze the legs as much as is needed, with a kick if necessary, slightly relaxing the pressure on the reins (but not losing contact). To stop him, squeeze the legs, straighten the spine and keep a firm grip. It may seem strange that one squeezes the legs both to stop and start the pony, but the secret is in the hands—they 'give' when you want to move off, but stay firmly still to bring the pony to a controlled and balanced halt.

To turn to the right from the halt, the right leg is applied noticeably behind the girth while the left leg stays firmly in place; the pony then pivots to the right on his off-fore. For a left turn the legs are applied in the reverse way.

When turning right on the move, the right-hand rein is used to guide the pony in the required direction while the left-hand rein checks balance and pace; the right leg maintains pressure on the girth, while the left is slightly behind, to keep the hindquarters on the same track as the forehand.

When cantering in a circle, the pony should lead with the 'inside' leg.

To make a pony go 'in reverse', which is known as the rein-back, he must be standing square, with a low head carriage. The legs are applied as if for the walk, but the hands, instead of 'giving', keep a firm pressure. The pressure of hands and legs must be even, for the pony should rein-back in a straight line with the head keeping the same position and no resistance.

When you have mastered all of these basics, *and it is no good going on to a more advanced move until you are completely sure of, the preliminaries*, you can take another big step forward.

PART FOUR

THE THREE SECRETS

Three of the most important 'intangibles' in riding a horse are balance, collection and impulsion.

The need for *balance* is clear. As already mentioned, the rider keeps his or her position in the saddle largely by balance, rather than strength. Balance must be a fluid thing, which alters to counteract a series of changing circumstances.

The horse, too, must be able to keep his balance, and it is one of the rider's most important jobs not to interfere with this. It becomes most vital of all when the horse is jumping. Yet it is only in comparatively recent years that the theories of a horse's balance have begun to be fully appreciated.

If you watch a horse jumping 'free', that is to say, without a rider on his back (*see* figure 18), you will see the way his head and neck stretch forward as he extends himself in an arc over the fence. This is because the neck is his balancing equipment. Yet in the past it was considered 'correct' to sit right back in the saddle as a horse landed over a jump, thus, obviously, pulling back his head. If it is seen now, in the hunting field or in show jumping, it is more often than not due to the rider's

Figure 18: Jumping free

insecurity in the saddle, and he or she is using the reins like a safety-strap, as though travelling on a bus.

Collection, like many words, means different things to different people. So a person who wants a horse that is well trained for ordinary work, perhaps as a hunter, may look at a high school dressage horse with its apparently restricted paces and decide that 'collection' is not what he or she wants. And certainly a hunter or show jumper would gain nothing by being trained to the degree of collection that is necessary to win a high award for dressage, but a certain amount is essential.

R. S. Summerhayes, once one of Britain's most accomplished horsemen, in his *Encyclopaedia for Horsemen* described a horse as being collected 'when ridden well up to its bit, with its neck flexed, jaw relaxed and hocks well under it, and, having full control over its limbs at all paces, is ready and able to respond to the signals or aids of its rider'. Which is what we all want when we ride a horse.

Impulsion, which is too often mistaken for speed, is rather like the spring of a clockwork motor. When a horse has impulsion it may be almost at a standstill, but it is ready to leap into action at the moment of command from its rider.

It is seen at its most effective and dramatic in top-class show jumping. A horse may come into a combination fence, which is one with two or more separate fences, at no more than a hack-canter, but, because it has impulsion, be able to jump clear over each fence; while another may come into the fence at three times the pace, lose its impulsion after the first or second parts, and stop.

For a show jumper, impulsion is essential, but for any horse or pony it is a great asset, the difference between a sloppy, slouching sort of ride and an invigorating, brisk one.

Projects

Observe and take notes

Take your camera to your riding school and ask the instructor if you can take pictures of a pony jumping free.

Take notes at your next gymkhana or when watching show jumping on television. Note why you think some competitors failed at combination fences.

PART FIVE

LEARNING TO JUMP

For many people the most exciting thing about learning to ride *is* jumping. It can be fun anyway, jumping over a ditch or a fence on your own two feet, but how much more so on the back of a pony, soaring into the air, imagining you are a jockey going over Beecher's Brook in the Grand National. Necessary too, if you want to be able to wander around the countryside without being held up every time you come to a fence where there is not a gate.

But, like everything else you have learned, patience is the word. Take things slowly and methodically. You will certainly start at the bottom—on the ground, in fact. For the first obstacle you will 'jump' is a pole, flat on the ground, or raised no more than a few centimetres, just enough to make your pony take notice.

When a pony jumps correctly he should arch his back, and this is learned, and something you must get used to, at the very earliest stage.

Then you progress to a series of poles, laid either on the ground or just a few centimetres above it, which are called *cavalletti* (*see* figure 19), a name from Italian, meaning 'little horses'.

The most useful type of cavalletti are those that have

poles fixed to crosspieces so that the poles can be placed at different heights according to the horse's and rider's stage of advancement. They will be placed about

Figure 19: Cavaletti

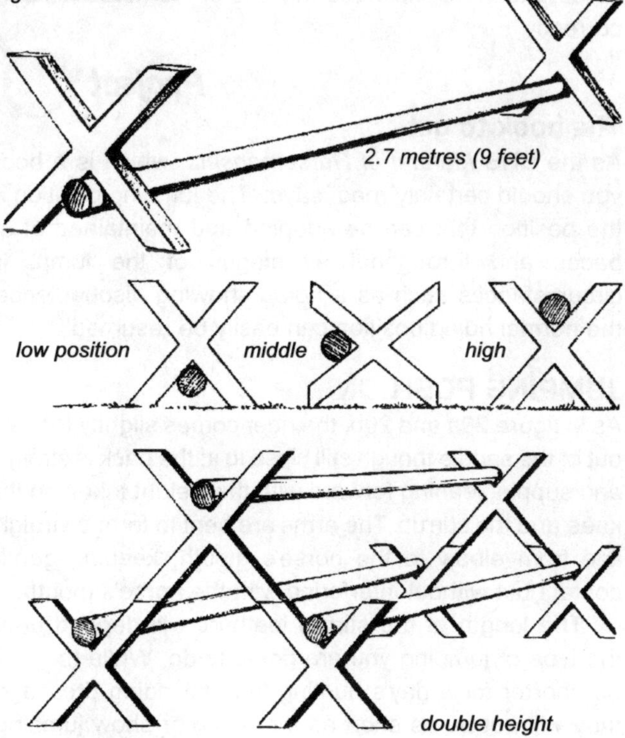

1.2–1.5 metres (4–5 feet) apart. And of course bigger fences can be built by placing cavalletti on top of each other.

Many learners put far more effort into jumping than is necessary. Usually the less the rider interferes with his horse, the more likelihood there is of the horse jumping correctly.

Project

The book to get

As the BHS *Manual of Horsemanship*, which is a book you should certainly read, says: 'The jumping position is the position that can be adopted and maintained at all paces and throughout all stages of the jump. In circumstances such as a horse showing disobedience, the normal riding position can easily be resumed'.

JUMPING POSITION

As in figure 20a and 20b, the rider comes slightly forward out of the saddle though still close to it; the back is straight and supple, leaning forward with the weight taken on the knee and the stirrup. The arms are bent to form a straight line from elbow to the horse's mouth, keeping gentle contact but without interfering with the horse's mouth.

The length of the stirrup leathers will depend upon the type of jumping you are going to do. While they will be shorter for a day's hunting than for riding dressage, they will not be as short as for racing or show jumping,

Figure 20a: The jumping position, 1 and 2

1 approach

2 take-off

Figure 20b: The jumping position, 3 and 4

3 over

4 landing

which would be uncomfortable for long periods. It is obviously impossible to say that they should be so many centimetres long for one sport and so many for another; this will depend upon a number of factors, not least your own size, and can be found out only by trial and error.

Over small fences the rider is nothing more than a passenger, and his or her most useful contribution is not to get in the way. If the horse approaches at a rhythmic stride he will measure the jump for himself, and the rider's main concern should be to keep in balance with the horse by maintaining the jumping position and not slipping back, which would place the weight where the horse would find it most difficult and at the same time probably jag at the horse's mouth, upsetting both his confidence and his balance.

Project

Learn to see the stride

Over bigger fences the rider can make a more positive contribution by the regulation of impulsion and stride in the approach. The difference in even the top class of show jumping between those riders who can 'see a stride' and those who cannot is remarkable.

As far as the rider's contribution is concerned, the most important part of the jump is the approach. If a horse takes off from the right spot, then there is every reason to expect that he, and his rider, will arrive smoothly at the other side. On a well-trained horse a rider can take up the jumping position for the approach, but if the horse is green (inexperienced) or a reluctant jumper, the rider must keep slight contact between his or her seat bones and the saddle to be able to regulate impulsion and stride as well as encouraging the horse.

Whatever adjustments the rider may have to make to the horse's stride and pace on approach should always be made at the last three strides from the fence to be jumped. The final strides are necessary for the horse to make his own measurement of the jump. Any last-minute alterations will only confuse him and probably result in either a refusal or a bad jump.

As has already been said, nothing is more likely to put a horse or pony off jumping than being jagged in the mouth every time he leaves the ground, and this is often seen among novice riders who, unaccustomed to the strange sensation, grab every available support to help maintain their balance. The only answer is a strong and independent seat.

Project

Find a jumping lane

If the riding school you are learning at has a jumping lane, this will be a great help. A jumping lane (*see* figure 21) is one enclosed on each side by a fence or hedge, with the jumps at intervals along it.

Figure 21: Jumping lane

The jumps need not be high, and, with no need to guide the pony, you can be sent along it without reins and hands on hips (*see* figure 22), helping you to learn to sit securely without relying on the reins for support. A regular practice of riding, especially at the trot without stirrups, is a good way of strengthening the seat, and eventually you should be able to ride along a jumping lane without either reins or stirrups.

Several years ago, in the practice ring at the Royal International Horse Show when it was at the White City, Harvey Smith, a showman as well as a brilliant natural horseman, watched for some time several top foreign riders who were schooling their horses very precisely. Then he brought his veteran Warpaint back to the

Figure 22: A jumping exercise

practice ring bareback and with only a headcollar on asked his groom to put the fence up to 6 feet (1.8 metres), popped easily over it and then rode back to the stable.

It will take a long, long time before you will be able to perform a similar feat so casually, and possibly it will never happen, but patience and concentration and a lot of training should certainly take you along the right path.

PART SIX

THE FUN OF TREKKING

New horizons open up for you once you are reasonably competent in riding and looking after ponies, whether you have your own or hire one.

There are a number of horse-related sports in which you can participate, such as show jumping, gymkhanas, hunting and trekking. Trekking is one the most accessible and most fun.

Even these days there are parts of Britain impossible to reach by car. To see them you need either to walk or ride, and naturally, as a pony can walk faster than a person, you can see more of the countryside from his back.

Pony trekking covers a wide variety of activities. It can be divided into three main headings: one-day (or even half-day) treks from one centre, returning each evening and then setting out again the next day, gradually covering all the area around that particular centre; long-distance treks, starting and ending in the same place, lasting perhaps several days, stopping in a different place each night, organised well beforehand and with the overnight equipment for pony and rider being transported by an adult with a car or lorry; and mounted expeditions covering longer distances and completely self-contained.

The first type is particularly suitable for beginners. In fact, a lot of people who have never ridden at all go on holidays like this, and because the pace is slow they soon settle into the unusual rhythm of the saddle. But, like most activities, if you have had some experience before you go, you will enjoy it all the more.

Project

Decide where to go

The first thing to decide is which part of the country to go to. The magazine *Horse and Hound* publishes a list of trekking centres each year, and the Welsh and Scottish Trekking Associations will also be able to help you. Ireland is a beautiful country for any sort of riding, and because it has so much open country is ideal for trekking. There are opportunities to trek in countries in mainland Europe, but perhaps it is best to start in Britain.

Probably when you have been going on holiday by car or train you have passed through an area, say the New Forest, and thought how much you would like to see more of it. Trekking is the ideal way.

Choosing a centre where you can be sure of having the right ponies, which are strong and fit enough to stand up to day after day of trekking over often rough and hilly country, is most important. There are many good centres, and some bad ones, where the ponies may be too young or old, or just not up to the job, and the 'instructors' people with only a minimum of experience and knowledge of that area of the countryside.

One thing to remember is that in trekking the cheapest centre is almost certainly not the best one. Buying, feeding and looking after ponies, and keeping them equipped with the best saddlery, is an expensive business, and a centre that offers low-price holidays, unless it is subsidised, will almost certainly be cutting its prices at the expense of the pony. It is therefore important to do some homework before choosing a centre, for your own safety.

Project

Get up a party

If you belong to the Pony Club and have your own pony, or if your riding school has a few people interested in hiring the ponies they ride regularly and making up a trekking party, you can be much more independent. Of course, the planning is that much more involved but this is part of the interest.

In this case you can decide whether you want to be based in one place and make day treks or to start off from one place, to which you may have been taken by horsebox, and do a circular tour, ending up after maybe four or five days back where you started, but with a much clearer idea of the countryside and the life that goes to make it.

If you are going on a circular tour you will need to ask an adult to drive the horsebox and to transport the bulk of your camping equipment by road to each night's stopping point.

MAP YOUR TREK

Once you have decided which area you want to go to, buy a map, preferably a large-sale Ordnance Survey map, and work out your route. You should allow for an average of say, 20 miles a day, although this will depend upon the age and experience of the riders and the strength and capabilities of the ponies.

To a large extent your route will be dictated by where you intend to stay overnight—perhaps in a tent, at a farm or a Youth Hostel, if there is one with nearby accommodation for the ponies. Looking after the ponies must always be your first consideration, for they are carrying you over the countryside, and the least you can do is to make sure that wherever you stop there is ample water and, if possible, good grazing and maybe a barn where they can be stabled (*see* figure 23).

The ponies' short feed, corn or nuts, can be carried in the car or lorry that is transporting your own bulky equipment—tents and so on.

Project

Check first

As well as the map you should, unless you are already experienced in map-reading, buy a book that tell you how to do it. A distance that may at first sight to the inexperienced eye look fairly short can turn out to be much longer and involve hills and streams and other difficult or impassable obstacles.

Many Ordnance Survey maps mark bridle paths, but it is always a good idea to check that these are still open and usable with local authorities, farmers and Forestry Commission officials.

When your expedition is not a trek that is organised by a centre, even if you are being supervised by a very experienced rider, it is always a good idea after planning your route very carefully to tell someone not involved in the trek about it before you set off.

Project

Have a look

This preparation may necessitate a personal visit or letters well beforehand to check on the route and to reserve accommodation for riders and ponies.

At the same time you must be preparing yourself and your pony for the trek. Write to the Pony Club asking for booklets on pony-trekking and mounted expeditions.

Figure 23: Pony tethered

These will be very valuable in telling you of some of the necessary preparations and what you will need to take with you.

Project

Prepare your pony

The pony must be given enough regular walking and trotting exercise to harden him up for the job, preferably with the equipment that you will need to take with you. Even if the heavy equipment is to be transported for you, you will still have to carry food for yourself and the pony during the day.

If you live in a fairly open part of the country, practise

your map-reading so that when it becomes necessary you will already have some idea of what to look for.

Project

Use a compass

Practise, also, with a compass, so that if you get into some particularly wild part of the countryside with no outstanding local feature, like a church steeple, you will still be able to track your path without getting lost.

It is a good idea, too, to buy a good guidebook of the area you are going to, which will tell you of the local pitfalls to look out for—such as the bogs and clay holes (often found in the middle of riding tracks) in the New Forest.

These 'circular treks' have the safeguard of an adult with transport to fall back on in case of accident—if possible with a horsebox or trailer in case a pony goes lame.

Project

Only for the expert

Completely self-contained mounted expeditions require even more detailed planning, not so much about the route, for you may be prepared to look for overnight stops as you go, but in the equipment you will take and the way it is carried.

These are, obviously, the most adventurous form of pony treks and even qualify for the Duke of Edinburgh Award Scheme. They are only suitable for those of you who are competent both at riding and in looking after your pony.

You must know something not merely of the day-to-day routine of feeding, watering, grooming, tack-cleaning and so on, but also what to do in an emergency. For this reason groups, though they should not be too big, should not have fewer than three riders, so that, if one rider or pony is hurt, another can stay while the third goes for help.

Project

Practise packing

Jeans and jerseys may be worn for ordinary short treks and are in many ways preferable to more conventional riding clothes. For mounted expeditions in which you will be much longer in the saddle, for perhaps 25 miles a day, jodhpurs are needed. The *Pony Club Guide* is very useful in detailing the clothes needed and also goes into some detail about packing (*see* figure 24). This is something that should certainly be studied and practised before you set off.

Figure 24: Canvas bag

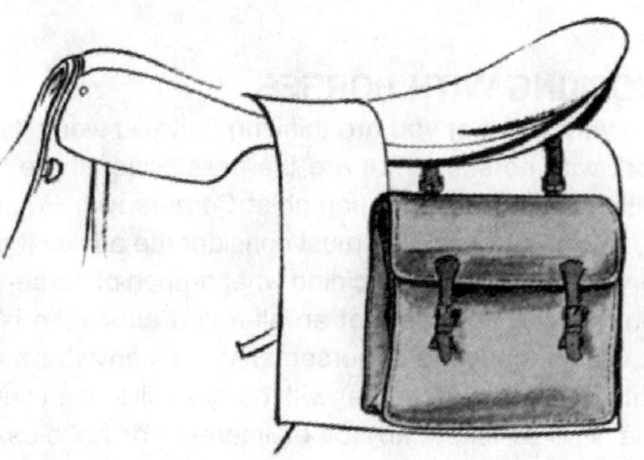

Project

Keep a log

Part of the greatest enjoyment of trekking is in exploration of the countryside, so keep a log of what you see and of your experiences, possibly starting from the time you first plan your expedition. Your experiences may prove useful to others when they do the same thing.

PART SEVEN

WORKING WITH HORSES

Possibly some of you are thinking that you would like to work with horses. What are the possibilities there? The British Horse Society's pamphlet *Careers with Horses* is a useful guide, and you must consider the advice it gives very carefully before deciding what branch of horse-work you fancy. It advises that an all-round education is just as vital in the world of horsemanship as anywhere else. It also warns that a career with horses will leave you with little time to follow any other interests or hobbies. You should also be aware that what can be fun to do when you want, at weekends or during holidays, can become a drudge if you *have* to do it every day in all weathers.

Project

Get a holiday job

So, before you decide to make working with horses a career, see if you can get some holiday stable-work, preferably during the Christmas holiday when the weather is likely to be poor and there are so many distractions.

Weigh up the advantages and disadvantages of such a life. If parties and enjoying yourself are what matters most to you, with the glamour of riding in the show ring or the thrill of a day out hunting as the highlights, forget about working with horses. The same applies if you want to earn a lot of money, for the chance of doing so with horses is small unless you are someone with the small build to be a jockey—and even then the chances of your getting a ride on the racecourse, let alone becoming a top-rate jockey, are remote.

But if, after all this cold water, you still want to work with horses, what are the prospects?

START STUDYING

The first thing to do is to study for the British Horse Society examinations. They are listed in the BHS pamphlet *Working with Horses*. The exams listed are primarily for those who wish to become instructors, but the BHS recommend that for every area of horsemanship the basic qualifications are the BHS stage 1 and 2 exams for which you must be at least sixteen years of age and a member of the society. The BHS Preliminary Teacher (BHSPT) certificate is the first certificate to be awarded to prospective instructors, and to be eligible at this stage you must be at least seventeen-and-a-half and have 4 GCSE passes or the equivalent. The Assistant Instructor's certificate (BHSAI) is the next to be awarded, then the Intermediate Instructor's certificate, the Instructor's Certificate (BHSI) and the BHS Fellowship certificate (FBHS), which is the senior qualification in the society.

It is also possible to obtain National and Scottish Vocational Qualifications in horsecare and stable management if your skills lie more in the area of horsecare or in running the stable yard than in teaching. Nevertheless, the NCVQ or SCOTVEC level 2 exam also provides a very good grounding for many different areas of horsemanship.

The Pony Club and riding clubs affiliated to the British Horse Society have their own tests, but these are a guide to ability rather than a qualification. So, for a serious career, the BHS examinations are an advantage you can hardly afford to neglect.

To get them, as with other professional qualifications, you will have to go to a well-staffed riding school, most likely a residential one. You may go either by paying a fee for a course over a relatively short period or as a working pupil, when you will be required to work as well as receive instructions. This will take you longer to pass your examinations. For more details write to the Training and Education office of the British Horse Society at the address given in Part One.

Project

Find out about training and career opportunities

Before you start training, it is important to ensure that the school you go to is of a high standard. Details of training centres that are approved by the BHS are available in the booklet *Where to Train,* which you can buy from their Training and Education office.

Project

Racing

Racing and hunting supply most of the jobs with horses. Work in hunting, except for the hunt servants, tends to be seasonal. Nearly all jockeys begin their training for their careers at Newmarket or Doncaster. Write to the British Racing School, Snailwell Road, Newmarket, Suffolk, CB8 7NU, telephone 01638 665 103, to find out about courses available for jockeys and racing stable staff. You could also write to the Training and Education office of the BHS.

Project

Grooms

Perhaps you could get a job as a groom. A groom is responsible for taking care of the horse's health and well-being. There are many opportunities for grooms in almost every area of the horse industry. The minimum qualification necessary is the NCVQ/SCOTVEC level 1 but, understandably, few owners will be willing to entrust their horses to untrained staff. Write to The National Pony Society, Willingdon House, 102 High Street, Alton, Hampshire, GU34 1EN to find out about qualifications available for those who are interested in working as a groom.

Project

Other areas to look at

The BHS's pamphlet *Careers with Horses* also includes information on specialising as a horse instructor and then taking this on further to work with the disabled in therapeutic riding, or as a sports coach for example.

There are many other jobs with horses. You could decide to work with polo ponies, in a riding school or in a trekking centre. If your riding skills are less developed than your ability to care for horses and in stable management, you might consider a job in a stud, which can be one of the most interesting and rewarding jobs. It is also possible to work with horses within the army and in the police force, but neither institution can guarantee that you will work in this area when you join as there are limited opportunities (this is especially true for women in the army). Or you might decide that the work you would most like would be in a more general field of working with animals such as a veterinary nurse or as a veterinary surgeon if you have the dedication and the ability.

Given the right qualifications, hard work and dedication, there is no reason why you should not succeed at whatever career you choose. By choosing a job that you enjoy, in a field that is suited to you and that you feel a commitment towards, you will have a much fuller, more interesting and rewarding career than many who go for more highly paid routine jobs.

PART EIGHT

EVERYDAY TERMS USED IN RIDING

Aged: over 8 years old.
Aids: ways by which a rider 'talks' to his or her horse, making it understand.
Bits: for controlling a horse. Reins fasten to the cheek rings of the bit, which passes through the mouth.
Bridle: straps attached to bit(s).
Canter: a pace in three-time.
Cast: a horse cannot rise again after getting down.
Cavalletti: wooden crosspieces joined so that a pole can be laid across at different heights or poles placed on the ground at intervals.
Cavesson: padded headcollar and noseband used for schooling young horses.
Cheek piece: part of the bridle to which the snaffle and bridoon bits are attached and which in turn is buckled to slip-head or head (top of bridle).
Colt: a male horse aged six months to two years.
Curry comb: a comb used to remove dirt and hairs from brushes when grooming.
Docking: the cruel practice of cutting the tail short to the bone, which was banned in 1950.

Dressage: the art of training a horse to absolute obedience to all aids and to the performance of certain specialised movements.
Filly: a female horse from six months to two years.
Foal: horse up to six months.
Girth: the strap that fastens the saddle on securely, running underneath the horse between the elbow and belly and attaching to either side of the saddle.
Hand: a measurement for horses. 1 hand = 4 inches (10 centimetres). The horse is measured from the highest point of the withers to the ground.
Hoof: the hard, horny part of a horse's foot.
Jodhpurs: popular dress for riding instead of breeches.
Lane: a narrow enclosure for teaching horse and rider to jump.
Leading rein: an additional rein used for schooling a young horse, leading novice riders or leading another horse when mounted.
Lungeing rein: a long rein fastened to a lungeing bridle for schooling a horse. The horse circles one way and then another.
Martingale: a strap preventing a horse from throwing its head up.
Near side: left side—the side that horses are generally handled from.
Pommel: the front arch of the saddle.
Roughed off: putting a stabled horse out daily for a

gradually increasing period to acclimatise it to the different conditions before leaving it out all the time.

Saddle: a leather seat placed on the back of a horse.

A standing martingale: (there are many types) a neckstrap supporting a strap fastened at one end to the noseband and at the other between the horse's legs, to the girth.

Surcingle: a girth passing round the horse's body keeping the saddle more firmly in position and preventing the saddle flaps moving.

Tack: a general term for all saddlery.

Tubed: an operation performed on horses with breathing difficulties. An artificial tube is inserted in the windpipe.

Withers: the ridge between the horse's shoulder blades. Horses are always measured from the highest point of the withers, situated just below the end of the neck.

LET'S INVESTIGATE!

Titles in this series:

1 Making Musical Instruments
2 Conjuring
3 Fossil Hunting
4 Being an Inventor
5 First Aid
6 Mapping the Night Sky
7 Ponds and Aquariums
8 Your Dog
9 Your Cat
10 Small Pets
11 Collecting
12 Painting in Watercolours
13 Tracing your Family Tree
14 The Weather
15 Drawing